On the Road of Love

Poems

Christie Leigh Babirad

ISBN: 979-8-8693-3090-1

Published in the United States of America by Harbor Lane Books, LLC.

www.harborlanebooks.com

On the Road of Love is dedicated to all the love that has altered, shaped, and colored my life story thus far, and has incomparably inspired my writing and desire to put pen to page and write directly from my heart's reality or imagination.

On the Edge of Love

Tangled in moments with you,

You've got me wholeheartedly embracing everything new.

My only wish is that you feel the same way I do.

I can't get you out of my mind,

Out of my heart.

The way you hold me,

All night long,

You give me a love I am aware some may never find.

New Love

One date,

A dozen talks in,

And I want to tell everyone about you,

How you already make me feel.

Trying not to send hearts.

Trying to keep my cool.

But I'm falling

Deeper and deeper

With each good morning and goodnight.

You have me

Spending

Sunlight and moonlight

Happily craving the next date with you.

The Fourth Date

Don't want the movie to end.

Don't want the lights to come on.

Yes, let's stay while the credits roll by.

Keep your hand enfolded in mine.

We feel so right.

And I can't help but reflect on our first kiss

A half hour ago.

Kissed.

Once.

Twice.

Three times.

Assertive and smooth.

Taking your time.

"Is it clear now that I am so into you?"

Before today, I did not know.

I was ready to close the book on all the possibilities,

Unfurling only this afternoon.

Now, I can't stop thinking of all the ways you touched me.

Hopes Up

It's too late.

Never takes much.

I've got my hopes up again.

There is no doubt.

And there isn't a single action to reverse these rising feelings.

Believe me, I tried,

With work and distractions.

It is no use.

My hopes are up.

Longing to see more of you.

Holding little moments in my head.

Dreaming for months ahead.

Praying you feel the same way too.

Knowing I'm already deeper in than ever before.

Knowing

This could all abruptly end.

Yet,

Continuing,

Like a kite

In the ever-changing sky.

Filled with desire.

Heart-pulled.

Blind.

Flying!

First Sparks

Almond eyes

Alive with desire

Looking into mine.

Electric beats

Pulsing through every vein of me.

And you hold me

Without any motion of leaving.

Present.

Exploring lands new to you,

So seductively foreign to me.

Who I Want to Be for You

I don't want to tie you down.

I want to be the one you fly with,

And the only one you desire to come back to.

When lists are pulling you here and there,

And you can't find a moment of peace,

I want to be the moment calling out to you,

The one who brings a smile to your face,

Ease to every part of you,

A reminder of someone who truly adores you

Without you having to do anything but feel what you're feeling.

I want you to be exactly who you are.

And at your happiest and most content,

I want to be the cause and reason.

A Sign of Goodness

When I am with you

Worries drift

Past the walls in the back of my mind.

I Need You

It's said that absence makes the heart grow fonder,

But be it a day apart,

Two weeks, or more,

I long for you just the same,

Losing myself in thoughts of you–

Reimprinting your lips on mine,

Retracing your hands on each side of me,

pulling me in closer to you,

Re-instilling the way your brown eyes read mine so well.

Ignited

Side by side,

The two glasses left on the counter.

Lips to lips,

The two hearts wanting to know more.

Body to body,

The two visions melding together.

Mind to mind,

The two wishes for this connection to last beyond this one night.

Away with You

Sliding into daydreams,

I don't need a feather of a nudge.

Floating away on stills of your touch,

Eyes sparkling

Reflections,

As you lean in to kiss me,

As I lean in to kiss you.

Deep Down

Deep down,

You should probably know,

I live in a Lionel Richie kind of love song.

That is when I am authentically myself.

Deep down,

In that place that reveals who I really am—

You will find all that I desire.

It's rather simple.

All that I desire is within that throwback sound—

The proven-to-have-stuck-by-each-other-in-the-most-
chaotic-of-times rhythm,

And the loving-each-other-the same-and-more-each-day
melody.

My soul alight with these songs filled with nostalgia,

Reminiscent of those sugar-sweet days—

Where I knew I was deeply valued and appreciated,

Within those carefree summer weekends on the beach,

Within those long day trip drives, with no set destination or
concerns of time.

No, I have never sought after power or money.

I'm only looking to feel alive.

I want to be forever loved.

And deep down

With each passing year,

My heart rises,

Too weary and too passionate to hide what I desire a
moment longer.

What I truly wish for—

It's a pure, unshakeable love,

Set to one of those classic Lionel Richie love songs.

Dear Billy,

I've been missing you.

If only I could send a letter up to Heaven.

Tell you how I met someone,

But I don't know if he sees me the way you used to,

With sparkles and magic.

You always told me I had more within than I realized.

You'd probably tell me to just give this love some time,

See where it goes,

Because at least it will be a story.

Oh, Billy, I think about you often,

How you saw life as a series of rich tales.

You chased down experiences.

You saw something intriguing in absolutely everything.

Christie Leigh Babirad

I'd like to believe you're still checking in with me,

Each Sunday like you used to,

Because I miss you,

And how you were all things belief and hope-filled for me.

.

Missing You

I'm missing you,

Like a two-in-the-morning-ready-for-dawn feeling.

I miss you,

Like the first day of vacation,

knowing you won't be here to hold me under the sweet Caribbean sun.

I've been missing you.

And with undeniable conviction,

I know my life will always be far greater with you traveling beside me.

What I Keep to Myself

There's a steady ache I carry throughout the day,

seeped in longing for you.

I have a constant fire flickering,

periodically fanned and bringing me to my knees.

I often go to the water on days like these,

but the deep blue and candy-pink sunset makes me think
of you.

You bring me such a romantic and at peace feeling when
you are around,

yet, I do not believe I could tell you any of this

when I still have doubts that your feelings are as deep as my
feelings for you.

Learning Curve

I've been told that finding "the one" takes a learning curve,

To master

The in-between,

Of flowers, candy, and compliments,

And,

Giving more than receiving in the name of unconditional love.

And,

Whether this one that you have chosen

Inspires,

Or,

Deflates,

Your precious spirit.

Protecting Love

Spinning away,

In a two-legged race of two tied-in love souls,

Neither wanting the naysayers to catch speed.

What She Wants

Kiss her.

And hold her tight.

The feel of you heals her.

Give her your heart completely now.

Love her.

Chivalry

Caring to protect her because you cherish her.

Holding doors open to show her that she is valued by you.

Initiating your affection for her.

Voicing how you emotionally feel toward her.

Answering her questions with honesty.

Loving her, especially when she is not loving herself.

Recognizing and taking action when she needs a helping hand.

Yearning to plan things you know will bring a smile to her face.

Navigating Love

There's no such thing as navigating love,

At least not according to any kind of plan.

Coming at you like a lightning bolt,

Making you move differently,

no matter how you try to keep the same speed,

Love has its own mind.

It's a no-map-traveler,

Taking you up and down,

To bliss, or ruin;

To always being born anew.

The Threat of Desire

It is the mystery that is the poison to the moment—

The other hand reaching out from the other room.

But we always have a choice.

To throw back the juice of intrigue,

Or,

Take in the sweet sustenance before us.

A Mistake

Never thought you would hurt me like this.

"I should have known better" is the refrain that plays.

Many nights I went to my dreams

With love

I never believed would be snatched away.

We used to talk.

We used to share secrets in the dark.

We used to care what each other thought.

Never imagined there would be nothing I would want to remember—

A lesson with no value retained,

Maybe only to never again open my mind and heart in this way.

Clarity

You wore the clothes of the open road,

But you were the dark honky-tonk hall.

You tried to convince me I was sheltered,

While a slideshow of stagnancy showed for you.

I was—

Glittered nights,

Passion and unwavering love in the everyday.

But you chose to throw it all away.

And for that, I am now grateful.

The Option

She's tired.

Turning the volume up on her phone,

All so she won't miss your call.

Feeling like an option.

Emptiness filling her heart.

This isn't right.

Shouldn't be like this.

Then she hears the ring,

And she's like a full amber-leaved branch

Protecting you from the bright sun,

Spreading sweetness and instant understanding across the
line.

She sinks into the moment.

Your laugh.

Your voice.

The joy and interest you temporarily show,

'Til the silence and lack of committed plans the next day.

Her left wondering once again,

How can she stop this wheel she's spinning on before you come back around?

This is Me

There's no watered-down version of me.

I don't sleep on it.

Maybe I should.

But I don't.

I'll tell you exactly how I feel.

Right or wrong.

I fall too fast.

And my soul's memory is often strung out way too long.

But I have no desire to change.

With this one life,

Sometimes moving like a three-a.m. bullet train,

I'm not the wavering kind.

If you're into switching from hot to cold,

What I've seen,

I have no other choice,

I'll turn off these emotions of mine as quickly as they come on.

'Cause I can't.

I can't be giving this full heart of mine to a simply-covering-his-bases kind of guy.

I've seen how this can all crash and burn,

With years of remodeling to keep the integrity of the original.

No, there is no watered-down version of me.

I don't sleep on it.

I'll tell you exactly how I feel.

And I am always prepared to take the wheel and drive off on my own,

Even when I really don't want to.

Messed Up on Your Kiss

I wish I could put you in the back of my mind,

Where I can't pull out the replay so easily.

I wish I could keep my feelings cool,

Not feel your mouth opening to mine,

Your lips on my lips

Kissing me like you mean it,

Like you don't want me to go.

My cheeks flushed now,

I'm aching to see you now.

Wondering why you can no longer keep a plan,

This mind of mine repeating questions I don't want to ask.

Don't you want to see me?

What happened?

Why did you tell me you were into me if you're not?

And I turn up these country men singing on my stereo
tonight,

Lyrics of missing the love they had.

And I lay back in my bed,

Continuing to write about the ambiguous subject of love,

Listening to the gravel and soul through the speakers.

Wishing—

Somehow,

Some way,

That is the passion you truly have for me,

That you are missing me too,

That I'm not just messed up on your kiss,

Denying the truth right in front of me.

An Inevitable Story

I know I'm feeling so much more than you.

Can't call it love just yet.

But I'm here counting down the minutes 'til we're together again.

And you've got me wondering if our souls will ever truly connect,

If one day soon you'll feel the same about me.

I know you have more heartbreak scars than I.

And I feel the block between us.

I'm trying to work my way through

With compromises.

Because I can't let go.

I can't give up on all that I do see.

And I can't become someone who pretends they don't care.

I don't want to be chill,

And I can't play us cool,

No more than I can slow down the fall.

Uncertainty

Keeping her mouth shut.

Not answering the skeptics' phone calls.

An ache presses behind her eyes.

She takes a few deep breaths.

Is what she is feeling irrational?

Maybe there's a reason he didn't text back.

I hope he's okay.

Turning up her music,

She writes down her goals for the following week.

And she repeats her individual accomplishments in her mind.

"*Stay on track*," she tells herself over and over again.

But,

She longs to be loved by you.

She can't stop recalling your hands on her face,

The way you looked at her,

The way her name sounded so sweet off your lips,

Completely right.

And she can't stop herself from jumping ahead,

Imagining every season with you.

Never Fall for a Writer

She has every detail

Whether you lay her down or not.

Your lips stay on her lips,

Your hands on her face,

Your fingers through the strands of her hair,

The sound of her name from your mouth,

The tiniest of moments you may not be able to recall.

Times pure and genuine,

She remembers them all,

Never fading in the slightest with passing years.

So never fall for a writer,

Unless

Immortality is what you desire.

A Writer's Heart

Sometimes a kiss is all we need,

And our minds are spinning,

Like a standing fan on a warm summer's day.

We move quickly,

With the purity and truth of a single moment.

Grabbing on tight,

Senses sinking deep.

Into dreamy lavender fields, we go.

Beckoning the healing haze to cover our entire beings.

Living within stirred and expanded feelings.

Images slowly sliding into future visions.

Strolling toward candlelit and fireside nights,

Red wine,

And soulful Christmas music,

turning round and round on a passed-down record player.

Losing Me

You're going to lose me

If you don't start caring more,

If you take my deep-hearted feelings as temporary emotions,

If you don't start spending your time showing me your love
is true.

I'm aware of the hard lesson you could be.

I'm hoping we can instead grow together.

I want to be the only one for you,

Like you are the only one for me.

You come so close,

But then I see you pulling away.

I feel that you're going to lose me,

And you will probably be surprised.

You haven't been paying attention

To the gentle signs,

The worry I have expressed to you more times than I would prefer.

You haven't wanted to listen.

You haven't wanted to understand.

And you really are going to lose me soon,

If you don't start caring more,

If you take these deep-hearted feelings as temporary emotions,

If you don't begin to spend your time actually showing me your love is deep and true.

Where is the line?

Where is the line

Between

You can do better,

And,

You don't see all that I see?

Taken

She's weary of being the one to deeply care,

The one who always reaches out,

Denying herself of what she needs,

Not wanting to be selfish.

She has been ingrained with moral teachings—

"Put others before yourself."

"Try to understand what another may be going through."

"Never react."

But all she desires is to be profoundly loved,

For a hand to want to reach out and hold hers,

For someone to really care.

Like a sunflower in the rain, she is.

She knows the showers are needed,

For sustenance and character,

But one too many downpours

Pounding petals,

And what was taken for granted will surely wilt.

Quick to Care

Quick to care,

Not to fall in love.

Most of us true love dreamers know the difference.

I'm quick to show him how deep my love can be,

But ready to leave if a lack of interest is what I feel and see.

I'm not one to waste my heart,

But give fully and genuinely from the start.

It is a lasting love I always plan for.

And no, I do not keep score,

But neither am I one to accept any sort of temporal lure.

To Write the Truth

I wish I could write,

Miss you so much.

But I don't want to add pressure to your heart.

I don't want you to ride in,

Like the prince you were raised to be.

I don't want you to feel you have to rescue me.

But I wish I could write,

How much I need your arms around me,

How I need your lips moving with mine,

How I can't fight the night tonight.

I wish I could write to you,

But instead, I tell you that I *understand.*

I tell you that *I am fine.*

I tell you lies to keep up the disguise,

To hide how very much *You have become a part of me.*

A Letter from Your Overthinker

Hello,

It's me again,

Your overthinker

Frantically searching for inner peace

To calm this crazy heart of mine,

Traveling in every direction.

I do try to hold myself back when I get like this,

But end up still needing reassurances from you.

You need to know,

I sometimes see myself as a full and lush pink rose.

But other times,

All I can see are the thorns—

An excessive Stephen King novel amount of thorns—

Do you see them too?

You tell me that you don't.

I wish I could see myself through your eyes

In times like these.

I don't mean to ask you the same questions,

Over and over again.

I know I do.

Sometimes the fire of doubt is all-consuming

If I don't have that grin of amusement and kiss from you.

I too often need to know—

Are we okay?

Did the joke I made earlier offend you?

Do you still love me the same?

Each time my overthinking takes over

I do try to be better.

But I need to be honest,

I'm going to need you to hold me tonight.

So please flash that grin my way

And kiss me slowly.

Please tell me you love me the same,

Through all of this overthinking of mine,

Between you and me.

Burning Bridges

We are advised to not burn bridges,

to not set alight to relationships that have scorned us,

to not make our exit irreversible.

But then I think about us,

and the way the sun shined,

over the wreckage,

the feeling of freedom that coursed through my veins

when I said my final goodbye to you,

overcome by a certain kind of joy,

like the break of pouring rain on the most humid
summer day.

And, months later,

when you strolled across my memories one afternoon,

I could have sworn I saw something—

A full rainbow,

wrapped around a tall, thick pine,

and with a flash of insight I knew,

walking away was absolutely the right thing to do.

Instinct

Sometimes you've got me feeling like—

I have too much going on to be with you.

Too much soul.

Too much Luther Vandross playing on my radio.

When you don't send hearts back my way.

When you have me wondering, how deep your love is.

Lately, my fingers run over that sequined red dress of mine,

the one that fits me just right.

And you have me ready to slip on those strappy high heels
of mine,

the ones I haven't once gone slow dancing in with you.

You have me ready to go solo,

out on the town.

You have me thinking too often,

of how I will say goodbye to you,

glancing at the cardboard box of old love notes I saved—

reminders.

But what I really want...

I want to feel free with you,

to be more, not less of myself,

and for you to tell me in a million different ways that you
love this woman that I am.

Boy, there is so much that I adore about you.

But one too many sometimes lately, you've got me feeling—

I have too much going on to be with you.

Too much soul.

Too much Luther Vandross playing on my radio.

When you don't send hearts back my way.

When you have me asking, how deep could your love
really be.

How Do You Feel?

On Monday, I believe I will be fine without you,

confident that it is time for me to let go,

that we were never meant to be a match.

But then Tuesday comes,

and I can't stop missing you.

You have my head spinning tracks of you—

every look,

every sweet comment,

every soft touch.

I think I might honestly love you,

but I don't know if you feel the same—

that's what keeps me from telling you so.

I told you,

takes two for me to be saying I'm unequivocally in love
with you.

You keep holding back.

Is this natural or purposeful?

I need to know.

I have a feeling you want to set the pace for our love.

But no matter which way we go,

fast or slow,

I've already fallen hard for you.

So that's why all I ask of you is for the truth.

What do you want me to do?

How do you want me to feel about you?

I told you,

I don't love anything or anyone halfway.

Motivator

I turned off the love songs today.

I'm feeling like the fool everyone has been.

I never thought being common would burn like this.

That was all I thought I wanted.

I convinced myself you were a wonderful asset to my days.

I believed you were motivating me to be the best of me.

Now I realize I had everything reversed,

upside down.

I created stories,

like I do,

all around the truth of you.

I bent and twisted the tales.

I made you represent what got me on my feet,

because I needed to do it anyway.

I let you be the goalpost in the distance,

but the moves forward were up to me.

It was always up to me.

Falling Out of Love

I'm falling out of love with you.

I'm closing up my heart.

Don't think of coming through with anything but a new start.

This isn't how a relationship should be,

You effortlessly tossing the ball back only because it went too far.

I Already Miss You

Makes me sad thinking about all I saw in you.

Breaks my heart to give up on you.

Because I know you can't see what I see—

Someone who was unwilling to let his walls fall down,

But also, someone I had cherished beyond all reason.

A Quiet Drive

Driving with no music today.

Only the sound of the wind and the road.

Steel gray sky above and bare-branched trees.

Soothing her hurried heart.

Allowing her thoughts to wander.

She got too used to the noise,

Washing away her views,

How she truly felt.

She needs the quiet.

She needs the silence.

She needs the music off,

To listen to the melodies

Humming inside her.

Where things are wrong.

Where things are right.

She used to take these silent drives all the time.

When did she stop?

For a long period, until today,

She would put anything on to distract herself,

To have some other voice in the room,

In the car.

Today is nice.

Today, this is precisely and exquisitely what she needs.

Why We Keep Striving

She does get tired of twisting the Rubik's Cube to see the patterns of her life line up.

She does become exhausted by this uphill climb.

It has been too long since she has felt a release in her mind and tight limbs,

And taken into her lungs the distinct crisp air felt only when having reached a peak.

But what greater choice does she have than to keep tenaciously pushing forward,

When love has always been behind her,

Rooting for her,

In one way or another.

This Heartbreak

Can you please tell me when the tears will stop?

This hurts beyond anything before.

Logic shows the list that proves you were never for me.

But I feel—

Such heaviness on my chest.

And these come-on-you-all-of-a-sudden emotions,

They take over my body completely.

When I know we couldn't have worked,

Why does my mind also show me the undelivered potential
I saw in you—

The hope of you realizing I loved you through and despite
it all?

On the Road of Love

On the road of love,

The sky continually changes.

Bright powder blue.

Sun-lit navy.

Pink and orange—

Creamsicle sunrises and sunsets

That seem to assure the spark is here to stay.

To the gray and obsidian darkness.

On the road of love,

We continually need to adjust our speed.

Through straightaways.

Side of the road waiting breakdowns.

Curves.

Sharp turns.

And up and down thick pine tree-bordered hills.

Her Choice

She backtracked,

Ran right back down that dirt road of memories.

The whole world can judge her,

See nothing but dust on the wind,

But they couldn't feel that beat in her chest

When she decided

She didn't want him to leave her town.

And they couldn't feel that peace

She felt

Every time he was beside her,

That instinctive knowing

He was meant to be,

Somewhere a being in her life,

In her story.

Lead Me On

Lead me on

To all you feel in this moment,

Right here, right now.

Lead me on

To my heart beating faster than it probably should,

Experiencing more than I ever thought I could.

Lead me on

To the moments that are wrapped in forever,

Memories that could never twist or sever.

And I ask you to please lead me on

To every dream you tucked away,

That you were ever too fearful to say.

Lead me on, my love,

To your soul that does not hold back,

Regardless of destiny and fate's track.

Our Place

A month deep into autumn

Overcast Sunday morning

Holding back the rain

On our deserted beach

We claimed

We're pulled here

Heavenly-guided

Magnetic connection

That drew us to each other

Desires never more strong

To stay here

Where everything about this moment is perfect

Everything feels right

And you say that you feel the same

Between sunrise and daylight

Sitting on a jean jacket

We have to get close

Nothing but miles of sand around us

Reading poetry to you

Misty ocean

A faded powder-blue sky

Even the seagulls have remained in flight

We're in the center of a story we are writing together

With your arms around me

Holding me tight

Instantly mending the week's breakage

Vision has never been more clear

With a faith-restoring light ocean breeze

In a place beyond complete

With kisses guaranteed to remain on my lips

To hold my heart when we must part from our place

Until next time

We make this promise

Defining Moment

When I, weary and consumed with doubts said goodbye,

And you paused

A few half-steps down the street,

Turned around on the darkest of nights,

Lit lamplights one by one on each side of my heart,

And said,

"Please, give me one more chance

To prove

What you feel could not be further from what I feel for you."

I Love You Too

It's on the tip of my tongue,

Aching in my heart,

Keeping me up with the replay of every date with you.

I tried to convince myself this is infatuation,

Not true,

Yet, I'm holding on tight to every word from you.

I have no trouble remembering

Every little thing you do for me,

Every place you have taken me.

I love you is on the tip of my tongue.

I'm aching to tell you that for me this is true.

But I wait...

On a sign,

Perfect timing,

To know this sentiment is not only in my mind,

That you feel the same way too.

Good for My Soul

He said *I want to see you. I need to see you.* I teased that I had forgotten what he looked like. He said that he hoped not, that I'm first on his list of plans. He probably wouldn't remember all that I've recorded in my heart, all the words that mean so much to me, that warm me in moments of crippling uncertainty and worries of which way the future winds will shift. He gives his heart purely, with such honesty. He is my steady place, but won't allow me to stand still. He wants the best of me and for me, and he believes in future pictures I can't always see myself. This man is good for my soul.

Technicolor Love

Bright as a moonbeam.

A love people place bets on,

Believing this is too good to be true.

But they lose.

Every time.

For the base is stronger than that of any fairytale.

It took a while to get here.

And most settle too soon.

This is a technicolor love,

Where the hues never fade—

Most definitely worth having waited for.

In Your Car

"Tunnel or bridge?"

It doesn't matter, baby,

I'd take any route with you.

Racing through city-lit avenues

Or 'round pine tree lined bends;

All I see is the way you quickly glance over at me,

All I feel is your hand enfolded in mine

Breathing in the exhilaration of never having been so alive.

For Old Times' Sake

On a windy day

At the beach you shared first dates,

You went there today.

"For old times' sake," you had said.

And she thought about this gift

Beside the ocean.

How sweet to have had old times,

To hold love close,

Beyond the changing seasons,

Through all of life's ups and downs.

Freestyle Love

I broke most of the rules,

The holding back in love experts say you should do,

All of what keeps a man supposedly interested in you.

Don't reveal too much of your heart.

Don't go handling their designated part.

Make sure he knows you have other options from the start.

I didn't want to play those games,

Didn't want to hold back from my interest in you

All to endlessly seek what's new.

It's true, I broke most of the rules,

What the love experts say you should do.

I guess it's pretty spectacular that we're a long-lasting match now,

Among very few.

Beyond Expectations

"I want to know everything," he said. A month apart, they came together on this first-hints-of spring day. A crisp wind swam across the atmosphere, but a bright yellow sun shone with newly found purpose. This man next to her wasn't a man to seduce with constant flattery and compliments. This at times made her doubtful of the depths of his feelings for her. But in his car, on this warmer than normal February day, her heart in a moment's time was as clear as the sun breaking through winter's heavy cloak. He said, "I want to know everything. What did I miss while we were apart?" And within his penetrating brown-eyed gaze looking into her eyes with genuine interest, she was given a heavenly touch of both peace and joy, knowledge that this love was as real as the return of sun-kissed skin. This love was true, beyond what she expected love to be.

February

The sun continues to set too soon.

The air carries a bitter winter chill still.

But there's something about February.

She can hear the saxophone clearer now.

Her mind is traveling again now,

To the warm breezes on a smooth jazz melody.

She can actually smell the sweet sun on days like these,

Moving to a Samba beat beside the sea.

She's seeing silky ruby red,

Watermelon kisses that stay on the lips,

Strappy high-heeled nights,

With white candles

And roses in every color,

And chocolate.

Deeper in Love by the Day

Let's turn back the clock.

Reach on over for my hand like you do,

As you drive us anywhere

In the sunshine or rain;

I'm falling deeper in love with you every day.

You make me so happy.

I feel beautiful when I am around you.

Your playfulness has me always smiling.

And when I am not with you,

You still move across my heart.

I need for time to stop.

Christie Leigh Babirad

I can't get enough of your soft touch,

As you drive us anywhere you want to go,

Your hand so sweetly in mine;

I'm loving this falling for you deeper by the day feeling I have with you.

Angel in the Wings

You need to believe in yourself.

You need to be self-inspired.

But isn't it sweet when you have that one someone

Behind the curtain, Waiting in the wings,

Ready to take your hand, Pull you into a kiss,

And tell you,

"Baby, I knew you could do this all along;

I'm so very proud of you."

He Feels like Sunshine

His presence feels like sunshine, she says.

Through her hair,

Tickling the nape of her neck,

Around her body,

Her heart,

Her shoulders,

Down her back.

And he knows how to hold me so right, she says.

Her previous worries evaporate fluidly,

Not in a rush.

With eyes wide open;

She is reminded of what is real,

What matters most of all.

He is not a shelter,

He is a home.

Mending the broken glass,

Genuinely marveling at how the light shines

Much brighter,

More colorfully

Through the cracks.

He feels like sunshine. She contentedly smiles.

He warms her soul.

And he is the inspiration for her continual growth into being more, not less, of herself.

A Moment

"Let me walk you to your car," he says.

Side by side we make our way.

Not saying much at all.

Past his car to mine.

Heart-full.

Feeling valued.

He thanks me for coming to meet him today.

He places his hand gently on my back.

And he leans in for the sweetest goodbye kiss.

Making this one of those moments that last beyond the moment,

To me needing to hold onto this soft and simple memory in this poem of mine.

Pristine

"Pristine"— a term that can be viewed differently, person to person.

For me, "Pristine" represents a sacred love.

Not symbolizing perfection, but rather an unwavering connection,

Never soiled by deceit or change of heart.

And I would say, with deep gratitude,

By my definition,

Our love is "Pristine" for sure,

Like the cascading and rushing with life waterfall beside us at this sunset hour.

In My Feelings

In my feelings tonight.

Thinking about how you reached behind me to open the car door for me.

Replaying, the sensation of wholeness when our bodies met,

When you leaned down to kiss me.

Reflecting, on the look in your bright brown eyes,

Penetrating my soul,

When you wanted to make sure I was okay after the week I had and shared with you.

I am undeniably wide awake, in my feelings, dreaming tonight;

Thinking,

Knowing,

I am totally, completely, and unequivocally in love with you.

You are my guy.

Fire and Water

A different sign found me,

and I like the way he moves.

He takes me to the water,

instead of the desert sand.

He shows me freedom,

with his fluidity in life's storms.

And, he calms the flames that at times ache with unbearable heat in my soul,

reminding me that I don't need to run to have all that I wish for.

In This Moment

Rain dripping down the car windows,

I gaze into your focused yet caring light-filled brown eyes,

Like toffee,

On me.

I tell you that I must be out of my mind,

Feeling all these feelings for you,

Needing you the way I do.

But I realize,

I am not being true.

For every date with you,

I feel a little less out of my mind,

More,

I can't imagine myself being anywhere else

In this place and time.

Good Morning

When the sunlight pours in through your windows,

how sweet it is to be your first thought.

I will never tire of this.

My soul ignites each day with your "morning" to me.

Simple as this may be,

It means a whole lot to me.

This is something I have always wished for.

To be thought of.

To be in someone else's heart and on someone else's mind.

I can't think of anything sweeter.

Fool for Love

At the end of her days

Let her memoriam say—

She loved.

She loved even when she didn't receive the same in return.

She loved to never close a door.

She loved for the expression of her own heart,

To never hold back

Sentiments she was pulled to share.

Some may say she was a fool at times,

But what greater flaw is there to possess

Than to never withhold the energy,

The hope that beats in all of us?

For it is the genuine love she has given

That has led her

To never truly break.

Acknowledgments

Thank you to my family and to the love and experiences that have come into my life thus far. As I always say, there is not a single being in this world who is self-made. Thank you to everyone who has come in and out of my life, and especially thank you to those who have believed in me and my dreams. Thank you to Harbor Lane Books for publishing this work that, as with all of my works, is so very close to my heart.

About the Author

Christie Leigh Babirad is an award-winning author of fiction and poetry. She is also a reporter and freelance writer.

Christie Leigh believes we all have many unique purposes in this life, the greatest one being "to love" and to follow that which stirs the heart.

She adores her family, which includes a spunky Jack Russell Terrier, Alistair, who likes to don sweaters and fancy collars in the chillier months. She credits her family, friends, and fans of her work for inspiring her craft, and that is one of the many reasons why she will always say that there is no such thing as being "self-made." She strongly feels that we are a collection of the people who have come in and out of our lives and placed love and belief in our hearts.

The primary hope she has for her readers is that her words and stories comfort and inspire them, letting them know that they are never alone. She wants her readers to know that their feelings have a real place, and that this life can be so much bigger and grander, if we let love and optimism fully into our hearts. She also believes in an after-life and that we remain connected to the ones who have moved on to Heaven. She's a romantic and looks up at the sky often, marveling at its enormity and how the colors and clouds are always changing and the stars keep shining, no matter what.

All her books are available via Amazon, B&N, and through other major retailers.

You can follow her art on social media at the following sites to find out more about her latest projects.

Facebook @authorchristieleighbabirad

Goodreads @cbabiradauthor

Instagram @christieleighbabiradauthor

YouTube@christieleighbabirad1707

About the Publisher

Harbor Lane Books, LLC is a US-based independent digital publisher of commercial fiction, non-fiction, and poetry.

Connect with Harbor Lane Books on their website www.harborlanebooks.com, TikTok, Instagram, Facebook, Twitter, and Pinterest @harborlanebooks.

The Navigator
TAKING HOLD OF THE HEART'S COMPASS
POEMS
CHRISTIE LEIGH BABIRAD